YACHT PORTRAITS

YACHT PORTRAITS

The best of contemporary marine art

SHERIDAN
HOUSE

Published in the United States
of America 1987 by
Sheridan House Inc.
145 Palisade St., Dobbs Ferry, N.Y. 10522.

Introductory text: Fabio Ratti.
Editor: Karen Hoare.
Graphical layout: Alberto Conforti, Katia Marassi.

Photocomposition: Fototype S.r.l., Milan.
Photolitho: Fotoincisioni Bassoli S.p.A., Milan.

Printed in Italy by
Arti Grafiche Amilcare Pizzi, Milan.

ISBN 0 911378 76 6

INDEX

INTRODUCTION

There has always been a special bond between man and the sea, just as there has always been a need to transmit the strong feelings derived from the depth and intensity of this relationship in such a way as to arouse an immediate response in others.

This desire to communicate has for centuries found its expression in illustrations; marine art in some form or another has its origins in ancient history. In Scandinavia stone engravings of nautical subjects date back to some 3,000 years B.C.; indeed, archaeological findings prove that all ancient civilizations produced examples of this art form. Nonetheless, marine painting as we know it today did not come into being until the 17th century: the period which saw the development of merchant navies, the discovery of new tracts of land and water, the origins of the first yacht clubs and the first racing exploits across the seas.

The center of these new developments was Holland – great nation of seafarers – and it was natural that marine art should have been primarily influenced by the Dutch and Flemish schools before passing on to other countries as the balance of political and economic power, and, with it, naval supremacy and exploratory prowess, shifted.

The influence of the Dutch school was, nevertheless, very considerable. Even though it may seem strange given the proverbial seafaring tradition of the British, the birth of marine painting in England was influenced by two Dutch artists: the Van de Veldes, father and son. In 1674, they were nominated 'official marine painters' by King Charles II and went on to produce more than 600 paintings and 8,000 drawings between them: father sketched the outlines while son put in the color. Their Dutch style, which has served to inspire generations of artists and is indeed still detectable in many works which date from the end of the 19th century, is considered to be the starting point of the era of British marine painting which came into its own in the mid-18th century. While the Dutch school declined, English artists came to dominate the international marine painting scene right through the 19th century and up to the beginning of the 20th.

First the Dutch, then the British: the third, and last, important artistic wave as far as marine painting is concerned, came from the United States, a country where marine artists are currently prolific.

The development of the nautical map and an ever-increasing amount of trade by sea between the continents stimulated the fashion of collecting marine art in America where the growth of marine painting as an art form was quite free from European influences.

It is no easy task, given their number and the quantity of work produced, to classify the artists of the past just as it is not easy to pick out from among them the 'real' ship portraitists, who, often working on commission, painted with painstaking accuracy so that the vessels were easily identifiable.

The Van de Veldes painted without doubt an unequalled number of ship portraits, but they did not limit their efforts to this subject matter, as was the case with other famous marine artists who lived in the 18th and 19th centuries. Dominic Serres and Thomas Luny, well known at the time and highly rated today, were ship portraitists who alternated portraits of ships with scenes of the Thames waterfront and seascapes in general.

The 'true' ship portraitists, however, were intrinsically dependent on the ships themselves. Their renderings had to satisfy the pride of the shipowners or shipbuilders, but they also served as a fount of information for carpenters and sailmakers who were able to take their working measurements from the scales indicated in the corners of the canvases.

Perhaps the most famous among British ship portraitists was William John Huggins (1781-1845), although he has also signed numerous canvases dedicated to naval battles.

A greater specialization of artists became apparent in the second half of the 18th century, with the setting up of shipping companies and the mariners' tradition of commissioning portraits of their own vessels for a somewhat modest fee.

Thus, in the busy ports of the world, a new profession was born, often passed down from father to son: a ship was always portrayed in profile with the harbor it was visiting in the background, flag rippling in a fresh breeze and its prow almost always proudly raised. This proved to be the most gratifying and splendid period as far as ship portraits were concerned. These tended to be less 'realistic' than their predecessors but much more accurate in the execution of detail: a ship was portrayed in a winning stance, confident, wind in her sails, perched on choppy seas.

The Roux family in Marseille, the Gavarrones in Genoa, the Cammillieris in Malta and the Luzzos in Venice are some of the most famous names among Mediterranean artists who favored the technique of gouache.

But the list is long, and comprises the Weyts and Loos families of Antwerp in Belgium, Peter Holm of Hamburg, Jacob Peterson of Copenhagen and many others.

On the other side of the Atlantic, the most famous and prolific artist was undoubtedly Antonio Jacobsen of New York while in the East, where artists did not sign their paintings with their initials but with the name of the shop where their paintings were to be sold, the sole historically recorded exponent was Lai Fong, who worked in Hong Kong and Calcutta.

The end of the golden age of ship portraits coincides with – and it is easy to see why – the invention of the camera and the ensuing popularity of photography of the sea and marine events.

From the celebrated photographers Beken of Cowes – pioneers in the field – to Allain, Borlenghi, Garwood, Eastland and Neuman (to name but a few of the most famous photographers of yachting events of our time), much ground has been covered; but something has also been lost. The publishing market is inundated with books, calendars, posters and journals featuring perfect and adventurous photographic renderings of vessels and sailing events. But these illustrations are becoming increasingly alike and the artist's interpretation and the fascination for things marine risks being compressed as an image is reduced by the lens of a camera.

Hence the raison d'être of this book: a search for those who still continue in the Van de Velde tradition, who make their living from painting ships and the sea, and a presentation of their most recent work. We thought that there were only a handful of nostalgics left. But we were soon confronted by a bewildering and difficult choice of material featuring a whole range of subject matter executed in a variety of techniques and painted by artists from all parts of the world – all united by a love for all manner of ships and the sea, and an indisputable competence in their portrayal.

Our choice reflects the predominance of American marine artists today. It cannot even attempt to do justice to the impressive efforts of many of the artists whose work is sampled in this book, and we apologize in particular to all those whose work has been excluded: their work would merit an encyclopaedia rather than a single volume.

FABIO RATTI

PORTRAITS

B.Sett. 1885

PURI

GENESTA

Cant. ORLANDO . LIVORNO   REGIO INCROCIA

CORAZZATO   G. GARIBALDI   ∞   1899

le côté "tou pierre" part pour sa dernière croisière
morey le thiz 1988.

le cat boat "belle oie" au large et au ... longue moue, kathy rays 1976.

1983
marc JJberthi
RMYS
Souvenir d'été

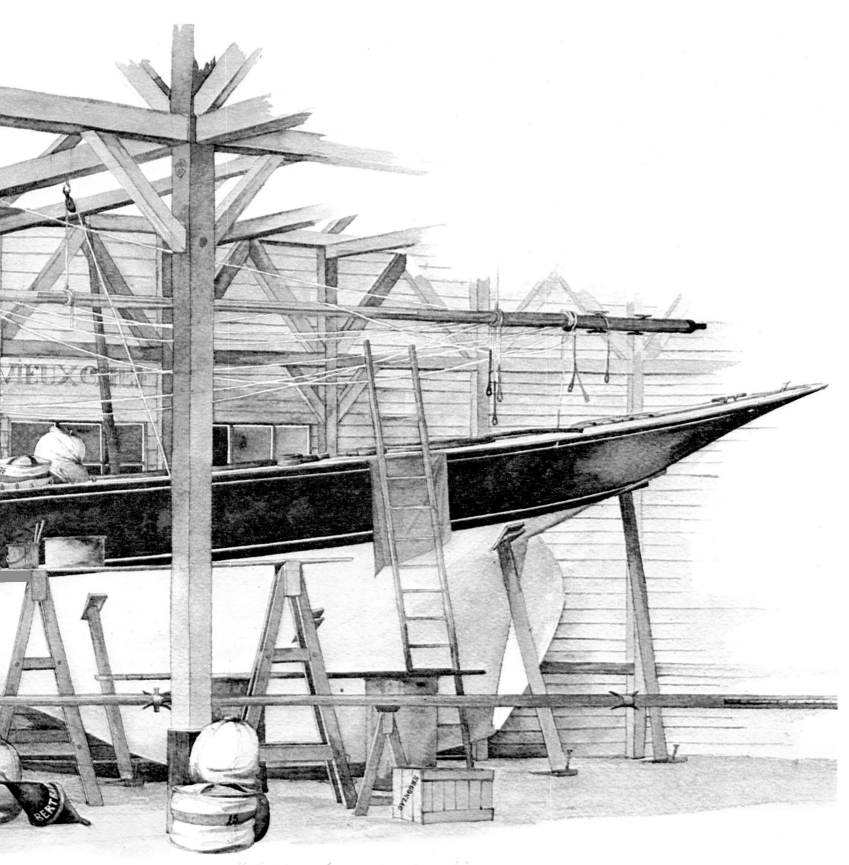

Le 6 mètres de jauge internationale
"Nouvel haute belle" attend le printemps
au chantier "Botine et vieux Clef"
Marie J.G. Bertrand Cospic Octobre 1979

© Gail Hunter Smith 1985

APPAREILLAGE DE BENODET

FIVEMILE RIVER AFTER RAIN

Royal George · Robert Stilker

BIOGRAPHIES AND CAPTIONS

ACCIARRI, ALFREDO

Born into a family of seafarers and small boat builders, Acciarri left his native Istria for Milan in 1944. There, he completed his artistic studies at the Scuola Superiore d'Arte at the Castello Sforzesco, working under tutors Consadori and Piantini. Initially an illustrator, Acciarri subsequently joined Studio Design Olivetti and worked under Ettore Sottsass Jr. In 1976, he began researching into 19th century marine art. The region of Liguria proved to be a profitable base for his painting career and he soon acquired the recognition of many personalities in the yachting world, frequent visitors to Portofino.

Acciarri, apart from creating his own art, specializes in the reproduction of 19th century ship portraits, displaying an inimitable accuracy of execution attributable to his knowledge of boat construction and marine technology in general. His mastery of color tonality and glazing techniques has rendered his paintings faithful documents of a time gone by.

Born in Istria, Jugoslavia, 1930. Lives at via Primule 18, Lainate, Milan (Italy).

1. *Puritan e Genesta*,
oil on marine plywood, 40 × 50 cm.
Genesta, *the English cutter belonging to Sir Richard Sutton and designed by J. Beavor-Webb;* Puritan, *The Eastern Yacht Club's boat, designed by Edward Burgess.*
2. *Incrociatore corazzato Gen. G. Garibaldi,*
oil on canvas, 50 × 70 cm.
The dreadnought Garibaldi, *constructed in the Ansaldi shipyard in 1899.*

ATWATER, JOHN

Sees quiet corners of New England in sharp definition and vibrant color, and paints each as a breathless, lush microcosm. Atwater's port scenes and small vessels are painted in acrylic and watercolor.

Atwater graduated from the Washington University School of Fine Arts. He is president of the Connecticut Watercolor Society, a director of the Connecticut Academy of Fine Arts and member of the American Society of Marine Artists.

His works have won awards in national shows such as the American Watercolor Society and Allied Artists of America exhibitions. In the 1985 Mystic Maritime Gallery International Exhibition, his painting of *Brilliant* was chosen by the curators of the Mystic Seaport Museum for their permanent collection.

The artist exhibits at the following venues: Mystic Maritime Gallery, Mystic; Canton Art Institute, Ohio; John Stobart Gallery, Boston; Mystic Seaport Museum, Mystic; Beth El Temple Exhibit, Connecticut; Greenwich Workshop Gallery, Southport; National Gallery, New York.

Born in Worcester, Massachusetts, 1954. Lives at 141 Reverknolls, Avon, Connecticut (U.S.A.).

3. *Alice & I.O.,*
1985, oil, 60 × 96 cm.
Mystic Seaport Museum.

4. *Early Morning,*
1986, watercolor, 46 × 68 cm.

5. *Brilliant,*
acrylic, 44 × 64 cm.
Mystic Seaport schooner, used as a training vessel for sailing enthusiasts.

BARBER, JOHN MORTON

Dedicated to the vanishing beauty of the Atlantic coast and the Chesapeake Bay in particular, Barber's work chiefly portrays the skipjack (the only commercial fishing boat in North American waters to still work solely on wind power) and workboats in general.

The artist studied fine arts at Virginia Commonwealth University in Richmond and paints primarily in oils.

In his efforts to document the Chesapeake Bay, Barber is an active member of The Calvert Marine Museum, The Chesapeake Bay Foundation, Ducks Unlimited, The Nature Conservancy and The Virginia Coast Reserve. He is also member of the American Society of Marine Artists.

Born in Leaksville, N. Carolina, 1947. Lives at 9013 Splitwood Circle, Richmond, Virginia (U.S.A.).

6. *The Skipjack Kathryn at Thomas Point,*
1985, oil, 80 × 48 cm.
This 1901 vintage skipjack is seen here passing Thomas Point Lighthouse. The cottage type, screw-pile structure was built in 1875 and still warns mariners off the dangerous shoal near Annapolis, Maryland.

7. *Twilight Harbor,*
1986, oil, 60 × 34 cm.
The last dredge boat returning at sundown to sell her catch of oysters at the docks of Tilghman Island, Maryland. Many of these wooden vessels are 100 years old and may not see another season.

8. *Windward Start,*
1985, oil, 56 × 28 cm.
Fishing Bay Yacht Club Spring Series 1985. The club was formed in 1939 and is headquartered in Deltaville, Virginia.

BERTHIER, MARC P.G.

Born on the Breton coast, Berthier was educated in the classics by the Jesuits of Collège de Saint-Malo. He went on to study at the Ecole des Arts et Métiers and the Ecole Nationale Supérieure des Arts Décoratifs in Paris. He simultaneously painted the scenes of many films, several interiors and exhibition stands.

Berthier took to sailing very early on, cruising and racing, particularly on 6 and 8 Meter yachts and has ventured "wherever there are buoys to round".

Since 1965, Berthier has written and illustrated dozens of articles for sailing journals such as "Neptune", "L'Année Bateau", "Yacht Club", "Die Yacht", "Connaissance de la Mer" and, especially, "Voiles et Voiliers" which he founded in partnership with a few old friends. He has written and illustrated five books, illustrated forty books by other authors and designed more than 250 book covers the majority of which for Editions Gallimard, a Parisian publishing house in which he was director of the maritime collection.

In the last few years Berthier has dedicated himself totally to sailing and painting for yachtsmen, shipbuilders and collectors in Europe and America. His preferred medium is watercolor and his subjects, coastlines, the sea and all sailing vessels.

Born in Brittany, 1944. Lives at 3 rue du Pont aux Cloux, Paris (France).

9. *Ton Pierre,*
1980, watercolor.
A Breton cutter putting out to sea on her last run.

10. *Belle Créole,*
1964, watercolor.
The broadside of a catboat.

11. *Summer Souvenir,*
1983, watercolor.
A yawl floating on calm hazy waters.

12. *Muriel Toute Belle,*
1979, watercolor.
A 6-Meter J class awaits the Spring in the shipyard Bobine & Vieux Chef.

BOEHME, NICKY

Portrays old fishing boats, cannery towns and the few remaining quaint harbors along the Pacific coast. Boehme's romantic style of oil painting often fuses an eighteenth century background with a twentieth century foreground.

Boehme studied technical art at the Oakland Art Institute and went on to become art director of several advertising agencies in Los Angeles. She has spent years sailing and studying the ocean, cruising through Mexico, Alaska, British Columbia and along the West Coast, so that her subject matter is authentic.

As a member of the American Society of Marine Artists, she has exhibited at Mystic Maritime Gallery in Connecticut, Newport News Museum in Virginia, the Ruth Carlson Gallery in Mendocino and the Lindsey Gallery in Carmel.

Born in California, 1938. Lives at 17301 Redwood Springs Drive, Fort Bragg, California (U.S.A.).

13. *End of Day,*
1986, oil, 40 × 56 cm.
Noyo Harbor, on the coast of Mendocino.

14. *Sea Spirit,*
1986, oil, 60 × 72 cm.
Newport, Oregon.

BOND, WILLARD F.

Translates his sailing experiences into big, bold watercolor compositions with all the exhilaration of contemporary yachting.

Bond studied at the Chicago Art Institute, the Art Students League in New York and graduated from Pratt Institute Art School. He then joined the U.S. Navy and acquired experience on battleships, cruisers and destroyer escorts during World War II.

For fifteen years he was a ceramic muralist and easel artist in Manhattan, whereupon he moved into a rain jungle by the sea in Jamaica where he experimented with geodesic construction. He moved back to New York in 1976 to work at the South Street Seaport Museum where he began painting ships and seascapes.

A member of the American Society of Marine Artists, Bond exhibits at the following galleries: Annapolis Marine Gallery, Annapolis; Arnold Art, Newport; King Gallery, New York; Noroton Gallery, Darien.

Born in Idaho, 1926. Lives at 61 Pierrepont Street, Brooklyn, New York (U.S.A.).

15. *Pursuit,*
watercolor, 78 × 55 cm.

16. *Candy Rig,*
watercolor, 78 × 55 cm.

17. *Bow Man,*
watercolor, 78 × 55 cm.

CESZYNSKI, RON

The works of this artist, executed in oil and gouache, are centered around the Great Lakes sailing history. Specializing in extensively researched nautical and historical scenes, Ceszynski has crewed many of the old boats he has painted. He is also illustrator and creative director for KCS Industries, Inc., Milwaukee.

The artist is member of the Wisconsin and Great Lakes Marine Historical Societies, Manitowoc Maritime Museum, the Nautical Research Society and the American Society of Marine Artists; he is locally affiliated with Landmarks Gallery, Milwaukee.

Ceszynski's most recent works were shown by invitation at the Milwaukee Harbor Exhibit in April 1987. He also exhibits at Mystic Maritime Gallery in Connecticut and at the Marine Plaza in Milwaukee. Many of his works hang in private collections throughout the U.S.A., England and the Middle East.

Born in Milwaukee, Wisconsin, 1936. Lives at 8325 North Lake Drive, Fox Point, Wisconsin (U.S.A.).

18. *At The Mark,*
1984, oil, 52 × 64 cm.
'Q' boats beginning a spinnaker run. Originally built for sailing on the East Coast; but many found their way to Lake Michigan. Quite a few still survive to this day.

19. *Sabre,*
1984, oil, 48 × 60 cm.
Formerly the sloop Estalena. *The late Romy Brotz of Sheboygan, Wisconsin, converted the 87-footer to a yawl in the late 1950s and won most of the Great Lakes races with her.*

CHAPIN, DEBORAH

Chapin's subject matter consists of a variety of racing yachts from small craft used in training children to sail, to large 70 foot maxi yachts raced all over the world. She is one of the few contemporary marine artists specialized in on-the-spot portraiture. Her technique is also unique in that she has taken an impressionistic approach to the subject, adopting colors and methods used by the French impressionists in application of paint to canvas.

The artist's work is published in "World Class Sailing" by Gary Jobson and Mike Toppa (1986), "The Dictionary of Sea Painters" by Edward Archibald and "The Yacht" magazine. Her collectors include the America II Syndicate, Thompson Industries and John Nuveen Company.

As member of the American Society of Marine Artists and the International Society of Women Marine Artists, she exhibits at Greenwich Workshop Gallery, Mystic Maritime Gallery, Kirsten Gallery in Seattle and Grand Central Art Galleries in New York.

Born in Fortcollins, 1954. Lives at 1319 Colony Drive, Annapolis, Maryland (U.S.A.).

20. *Laser Beams,*
1986, oil, 38 × 56 cm.

21. *Horizon Job,*
1982, oil, 45 × 63 cm.

DEMERS, DONALD

Demers began to develop an interest in the sea from spending summers in Boothbay Harbor, Maine. He attended the school of the Worcester Art Museum, Massachusetts, and concluded his formal studies at the Massachusetts College of Art in Boston in 1979. His education as a marine painter continued as a crew member aboard many traditional sailing vessels.

Demers' illustrations can be found in national publications such as "Sail Magazine" and "Yankee Magazine" where his works appear on a regular basis.

In 1986, he was selected to participate in the annual show at the Museum of American Illustration. Member of the American Society of Marine Artists, his paintings have been exhibited extensively by the Mystic Maritime Gallery at the Mystic Seaport Museum in Connecticut. His work has also been shown by the Greenwich Workshop Gallery and the Mariners' Museum in Newport News.

Born in Lunenburg, Massachusetts, 1956. Lives at 26 Whipple Road, Kittery, Maine (U.S.A.).

22. *Resting Her Bones,*
oil on panel, 48 × 72 cm.
Although essentially native to Maine, lobsterboats are seen all along the north eastern seaboard of the U.S.A. This vessel, of 1940 vintage, is pictured in Cape Neddick River lying on her side as the tide runs out. Even though she is helpless in the mud, her beautiful lines maintain her poise as she rests her bones.

23. *Portsmouth Tugs,*
oil on canvas, 96 × 144 cm.
Tugs on the Piscataqua River, Portsmouth, New Hampshire, in the 1920s. Square riggers, schooners and today freighters and tankers were and are helped along the river by these tugs and others that followed in their wake. In the foreground is a gundalow. These barge type vessels are native to the Piscataqua and were a common sight in earlier days carrying cargoes to and from river-side factories.

DEROSSET, RICHARD W.

Known for his painstaking accuracy in execution – from the exact number of portholes and smokestacks to the true color of a ship's weathered hull. DeRosset works from paper models of vessels to get the desired perspective and researches into the period of time in the vessel's career, weather conditions, location and the kind of work the vessel was employed in before putting paint to canvas. Most of his work is commissioned by the San Diego Aero Space Museum, the Navy Combat Museum in Washington D.C., the Smithsonian Institute and various steamship companies. With no formal art training to his name, DeRosset began painting between assignments as the captain of the 500-ton tanker *Pacific Trojan*. He has spent fifteen years at sea which includes five years in the U.S. Navy as an assault boat coxswain and quartermaster. Subsequently, he became a commercial fisherman, obtaining his master's papers.

A dedicated historian, DeRosset is member of the San Diego County "Congress of History". He is also member of the American Society of Marine Artists, the Universal Ship Cancellation Society and the Vietnam Veterans Art Association.

Born in Boston, Massachusetts, 1953. Lives at 5460 Connecticut Avenue, La Mesa, California (U.S.A.).

24. *The Statue of Liberty - Dedication Day, Oct. 28 1886*,
1985, acrylic, 48 × 72 cm.
Gala opening ceremonies were somewhat dampened by foul weather, but thousands of spectators filled more than a hundred boats that day; many of those present had travelled long distances to be included in the flotilla surrounding Liberty Island.

25. *The Final Hour, R.M.S. Titanic*,
1983, acrylic, 48 × 72 cm.
White Star's 'unsinkable' super liner and the world's largest, most luxurious ship of the time. The Titanic *was on her maiden transatlantic voyage when she hit an iceberg on April 14th 1911, and sank with a loss of 1,503 lives.*

E'DRIE, LORRAINE

An accredited art world personality and international traveller, E'drie paints many subjects with unique feeling and inspiration drawn from devoted experience.

Having drawn the subject, her technique involves first wetting the paper (3001b paper-rough imported from France) and then applying wet paint on top. This lets the white of the paper come through, giving a fresh touch to the painting. E'drie studied at Laguna School of Art, Pasadena School of Design and at the University of Irvine. She conducts an annual workshop at Asilomar in Carmel, California.

She is member of New York's Salmagundi Club, the National Watercolor Society, Watercolor West and the American Society of Marine Artists. Her originals and prints have been featured in "Southwest Art" magazine. She exhibits at the National Art Club in New York, Laguna Art Museum, Riverside Art Museum, San Bernardino Art Museum and galleries in Carmel, Laguna and Newport Beaches.

E'drie is commissioned by Barco Engineering, Bank of America, Executive Motor Home Corp., Church Engineering of Newport Beach, Orange County Board of Realtors, Gavin Herberts "Casa Pacifica" (The Western White House).

Born in Los Angeles, California, 1927. Lives at 1809 1/2 W. Bay Avenue, Newport Beach, California (U.S.A.).

26. *Coming Home*,
watercolor, 46 × 60 cm.
Resolution, *a three-masted schooner, built in 1800.*

27. *Bayside Sails*,
watercolor, 36 × 46 cm.
Newport Harbor.

EGELI, PETER E.

Born into a family of artists, Egeli brings generations of art experience and color sensitivity of an accomplished portraitist to his atmospheric views of working sail on Chesapeake Bay.

Although he does paint historical and contemporary yachts, the artist mostly portrays the wide-beamed, shallow-draft bugeyes and skipjacks which sail on the St. Mary's River.

Egeli's artistic training at the Maryland Institute of Art, the Corcoran School of Art in Washington and the Art Students League in New York gave him exposure to and experience with the different mediums he uses in his marine paintings and is partially responsible for his versatility and sincere lack of preference for any one medium over another.

Egeli won the Schaefer Maritime Art Award Trophy at Mystic Seaport's International Marine Show in 1981 and was gold medalist in the Franklin Mint's 1975 Competition for Distinguished Marine Art.

As charter member and president of the American Society of Marine Artists, he exhibits at the World Trade Center, Peabody Museum, Grand Central Galleries, Newman & Saunders Gallery and Mystic Seaport Museum Gallery. His works hang in many permanent collections among which Colonial Williamsburg Foundation, U.S. Departments of State and Agriculture and the U.S. Navy and Airforce.

Born in Miami, Florida, 1934. Lives at Westbank, Drayden, Maryland (U.S.A.).

28. *The Yawl Scherezade*,
1981, oil, 48 × 72 cm.
A custom-rigged Hinckley "Bermuda Forty", built in Southwest Harbor, Maine in 1971.

29. *Lazy Days - The Cutter Galatea*,
1974, oil, 48 × 72 cm.
A portrait of Egeli's own yacht with her first rig. The mainsail was made from an old Bounty main and the jib and forestaysail were recut from an old Friendship sloop.

Yachtsman and student of maritime history, English illustrates profiles of sailing yachts with a feeling of crisp clear air that evokes every sailor's dream of a perfect day.

Former student at the Trenton School of Industrial Arts and Trenton State College graduate, his early occupations included those of sign painter, cartoonist and draftsman. An inventor with several patents to his credit, English founded a manufacturing business utilizing his discovery of a new method of producing molded plastic parts. Upon his withdrawal from active business, he dedicated himself totally to his art.

As member of the American Society of Marine Artists, English exhibits widely. Five of his works have won awards, among which a gold medal in a national competition sponsored by the Franklin Mint Gallery of American Art.

Born in New Jersey, he moves between his summer studio on Toms River, New Jersey, and his winter studio at 210 Seaview Drive, Key Biscayne, Florida (U.S.A.).

30. *Atlantic,*
oil, 40 × 48 cm.
The American yacht that set the durable record for an Atlantic crossing under sail in 1905. Her success was due to what is now recognized to have been a rare combination of circumstances: a hull design and sail plan which was, by accident, near perfect for the job, a daring skipper (Charles Barr) and a weather pattern which happens once or twice a year, at unpredictable intervals.

31. *Suzanne,*
oil, 48 × 60 cm.

A Southerner whose ambitious panoramas of New England coves and harbors are remarkable for their detail and character of the place. Fraser's subjects range from the Southeastern Sea Islands of his childhood and Maine's coastal villages to the varied shores of the East and West coasts.

In his desire to preserve on paper the way the coast is now, Fraser believes he is painting for posterity. His concern with accuracy is such that no detail, however 'unaesthetic' it may be, is painted out. This does not mean that he paints precisely what a photograph may record since he often alters the perspective to increase the viewer's intimacy with the scene or rearrange boats to suit his artist's sense of balance.

Before focusing on painting, Fraser was an illustrator and graphic artist in Pennsylvania, having studied graphic design at the University of Georgia.

Fraser has recently exhibited in shows at Grand Central Art Galleries, New York, and Montgomery Gallery, San Francisco and won an award of excellence at Mystic Maritime Gallery's Annual International Exhibition in 1986. Juried New York City group shows he participates in are those organized by the Knickerbocker Artists, the Salmagundi Club and the Allied Artists of America, the last of which awarded him the John Young-Hunter Memorial. With the Mary L. Litt Medal, Fraser's work was recognized by the American Watercolor Society. He is also member of the American Society of Marine Artists.

Born in Savannah, Georgia. Lives in Charleston, South Carolina (U.S.A.).

32. *Stage Harbor on Cape Cod, Massachusetts,*
1984, watercolor, 48 × 76 cm.

Marine painter, composer, journalist and sculptor. Specializing in ship and yacht portraiture, Freje also paints the sea and small boats. As sculptor, his naturalistic works are characterized by a typically personal and rustic style.

The artist studied at Gothenburg University and attended the Swedish Naval Academy. He has exhibited at more than forty venues, including the International Antiques Fair, Salon Ecole de Paris, the Marine Museum in Karlskrona, the Gothenburg Maritime Museum, the Nya Varvet Naval Port and Western Naval Base in Gothenburg and the Balida, Smögen and Tångudden Art Galleries.

Freje's paintings may be found in private and public art collections world-wide, including Buckingham Palace, London, the Royal Palace, Stockholm, le Palais de l'Elysée, Paris, the Arlanda Airport, Stockholm and Novotel, Gothenburg.

Born in Gothenburg in 1920. Lives at Vanadisgatan 12, Västra Frölunda, Gothenburg (Sweden).

33. *A Shrimp Trawler Riding out a Gale,*
oil, 73 × 60 cm.
Original owned by Restaurang Valand, Gothenburg.

34. *A Ketch Sailing into the Light,*
oil, 73 × 60 cm.
Original owned by Restaurang Lilla London, Gothenburg.

GIBBS, LEN

Depicts the maritime scene of the West Coast in a unique style of high realism that merges fine art with impeccable detail, working in watercolor, acrylic and pencil.

While most marine artists paint seascapes or boats, Gibbs gives priority to people and their relationship to the sea – whether it be children playing on the beach or venerable mariners repairing their nets. His explicitly drawn images leave nothing to accident. Each painting begins with a broad abstract plan on which everything else is hung and the finished works reveal a complexity of detail with every nuance of texture, color and light painstakingly portrayed.

Raised in a small fishing community in Manitoba, Gibbs has an in-born affinity with the sea. Although he has drawn and painted all his life, he went full-time only eighteen years ago and is member of the Canadian Association of Marine Artists.

Gibbs exhibits at West End Gallery, Edmonton, Ingrid's Gallery, Los Altos, Royal Institute of Painters in Watercolour, London and Hollander York Gallery, Toronto. Most of his art is hanging in private collections, among which Shell Oil, Dofasco Ltd., Scott Paper Co., Pan Canadian Petroleum Ltd., Mendel Art Gallery, Gulf Oil and Canadian Northwest Energy Corp.

Born in Cranbrook, 1929. Lives at 1 Dunelm Village, 416 Dallas Road, Victoria, British Columbia (Canada).

35. *Lifting Fog,*
acrylic on board, 48 × 64 cm.
Pictured is the misty loneliness of the remote west coast of Canada. The weathered character of the yachtsman as reflected in the dinghy: an essential commodity since much of this coastline is uninhabited, without marinas or docks.

36. *Rounding The Windward Marker,*
acrylic on board, 48 × 64 cm.
Canada II, contender in America's Cup 1987 in Fremantle, Australia.

GILKERSON, WILLIAM

Scrimshaw artist and painter in watercolors, his present historical style is characterized by muted tonalities, a limited palette and interpretation of latter day ship portraitists Roux, Fedi and Toulza. Gilkerson is responsible for having revolutionized the traditional art form of mariners – scrimshandering – bringing it forcibly into our own century; his book "The Scrimshander" has served to cement his reputation.

Gilkerson's paintings contain a combination of qualities: spontaneity (based on on-the-spot sketches taken from life); a sailor's eye (having spent much of his life sailing on the family yacht *Elly*); a study of the old masters as a basis for his own renderings.

Years of writing have led the artist to an analytical understanding of the fundamental elements of art, as exemplified in the Peabody Museum of Salem's book "Maritime Arts by Wm. Gilkerson" and in "Artist's Remarks" from his "An Arctic Whaling Sketchbook". Gilkerson has held eight one-man exhibitions and his signed work has been commissioned or purchased by such institutions as the White House, the Whaling Museum of the Pacific in Hawaii, the Museum of Fine Arts in Boston, Hamburg Maritime Museum in Germany and the National Maritime Museum in San Francisco. He is a member of the American Society of Marine Artists.

Born in 1936. Lives at Hathaway Mill Farm, Rochester, Massachusetts (U.S.A.).

37. *Elly Sailing off the Swedish Coast,*
watercolor.

38. *Elly at her Mooring in Marion, Massachusetts,*
watercolor.

Elly *is one of the oldest yachts still in commission. She was constructed in Sweden in 1875 c. as a herring fishing boat, converted into a yacht in 1898 and has been in the artist's family since 1913. She is a 28 foot gaff-rigged cutter of 5 1/2 tons brought to the U.S. from Sweden in 1981.*

HÖLMSTROM, ERLAND

Hölmstrom's marine illustrations have been published in sailing journals such as "Les Cahiers du Yachting", "Yachting World", "Die Yacht", "Boote", "Sail" and "Segling". He works mainly in advertising, but also illustrates nautical books for the international market.

Born in Sweden in 1943. Lives at Banersgatan 2b, Malmö (Sweden).

39. *Spaekhuggeren,*
1976, watercolor, 50 × 70 cm.

40. *Dip-pole-gybe,*
1978, watercolor, 56 × 33 cm.

41. *Balling,*
1972, watercolor, 28 × 39 cm.

42. *Charisma,*
1976, watercolor, 55 × 30 cm.
American Admiral's Cup contender, designed by Sparkman & Stephens.

HUNT, PETER ALAN

Freelance marine artist and illustrator working in the New England area, Hunt specializes in miniature yacht portraits often created to be hung in the yachts themselves. His medium is graphite and prismacolor on mylar, a unique process the artist has developed to get great detail in a small drawing that is also impervious to dampness.

The artist was exposed to boats by his grandfather who was an officer in the Coast Guard Auxiliary and most of his childhood was spent in Southeastern Massachusetts in close proximity to Cape Cod, Buzzard and Narragansett Bays. While in high school he built "The Shed for Sail", his present work premises.

Hunt initially studied at the Massachusetts Maritime Academy and then began boatbuilding in fiberglass and wood, restoring highly varnished antique runabouts and "lake" craft. He went to Ricks College in 1982 to study art and illustration under the eminent American wildlife artist Leon Parson. Since 1984, he has contributed technical and airbrush illustrations to "Cruising World" magazine.

As member of the American Society of Marine Artists, he displays fine art pieces exclusively at the Mystic Seaport Museum Gallery.

Born in Boston, Massachusetts, 1958. Lives in Smith Street, Norton, Massachusetts (U.S.A.).

43. *Launch,*
graphite and prismacolor.
A 1905, 38 foot glass-cabin launch built by New York Yacht, Launch and Engine Co. She is currently owned by Fredrick Gariepy of Attleboro, Massachusetts.

44. *Steam Yacht Swallow,*
graphite and prismacolor, 31 × 22 cm.
Built in 1893 by the Atlantic Works in East Boston and spent most of her life on Lake Winnipesaukee in New Hampshire. She is currently owned by David Thompson of Moultonboro, New Hampshire.

HUNTER SMITH, GAIL

Painter in acrylics, Hunter Smith takes herculean pains with her diminutive harbor views to create a realism more than photographic.

She attended Memphis State University for one year, majoring in painting, and graduated with a BFA degree in advertising design from Memphis Academy of Arts.

The artist has had a varied career as designer and art director of various advertising agencies, as publication designer for Temple University, Philadelphia and as painting instructor of children at Haddonfield Art League. She is currently participating in the restoration of a classic wooden motorsailer.

Hunter Smith is represented by Mystic Maritime Gallery in Mystic, Capricorn Gallery in Bethseda, Alcie Bingham Gallery in Memphis and Julie Fletcher & Associates in Park Ridge, New Jersey. She is member of the Artists Equity Association, the American Institute of Graphic Arts, the Society of Scribes, the Society of Illustrators, the National Museum of Women in Arts, the National Association of Female Executives and the American Society of Marine Artists.

Her recent exhibitions include the A.S.M.A. show at the Arnold Art Gallery, Newport, and the Invitational, the Schooner, the Inaugural Exhibition and Small Craft shows at Mystic Maritime Gallery.

Born in Nashville, Tennessee. Lives at Barnegat Light, New Jersey (U.S.A.).

45. *The Regina M at Mystic Seaport,*
acrylic, 11.5 × 18 cm.

46. *Sailboats at Dock, Fort Lauderdale, Florida,*
acrylic, 17.5 × 17 cm.

HUTCHINSON, JOHN W.

The artist's subject matter is generally vessels that sailed New England waters at the turn of the century, racing yachts, tugs, catboats, pilot and fishing schooners, sidewheel steamers and a variety of common working boats that played an integral role in the commercial growth of the region.

Hutchinson had no formal art education but was influenced by 19th century marine painters Robert Salmon and F.H. Lane. He began working in acrylics in 1970 and was subsequently inspired by Winslow Homer's watercolors to turn to that medium ten years ago.

In 1980, Hutchinson became the first contemporary artist to have his work exhibited at the Peabody Museum of Salem. Member of the American Society of Marine Artists, he has also exhibited at the Mystic Seaport Gallery and his works have been purchased by the Peabody Museum, State Street Bank and Liberty Financial Services.

Born in Boston, Massachusetts, 1940. Lives at 44 Bayview Avenue, Salem, Massachusetts (U.S.A.).

47. *Catboats Racing off Marblehead Neck,*
watercolor, 12 × 39 cm.

48. *Maxiboats Racing off Newport,*
watercolor, 25 × 44 cm.

JAY, NORMA

In a style mid-way between impressionism and realism, Jay captures on canvas the sensuous, richly lit world of the waterfront. She has a predisposition for gentle scenes of slumbering boats in small harbors situated along the West Coast. Jay employs her intuitive awareness of the play of light and shadow in order to capture her fleeting, atmospheric impressions of nature. A free use of unmixed colors gives grace and elegance of style to the otherwise deliberate organization of her paintings.

Jay studied at the Art Institute of Chicago, California State University, Wichita State University and Laguna Beach School of Art. Recent awards include: first place in the San Bernardino Traditional Artists Exhibition; artist award in the Rancho California Invitational Art Show; best of show in the Ford National Competition.

A member of the American Society of Marine Artists, Jay exhibits at the Mariners' Museum (Newport), Mystic Seaport Museum (Mystic), Orange Company Marine Institute and Nautical Heritage Museum (Dana Point). Jay's works have been published in "Southwest Art" (Feb. 1977 and Dec. 1983), "Sea History" (Winter 1980-81) and "Bay Views" (Mar. 1979 and Oct. 1978) magazines. She is included in E.H.H. Archibald's "The Dictionary of Sea Painters" and listed in "Who's Who in American Art".

Born in Wichita, Kansas, 1925. Lives at 19501 Vista Plaza, Laguna Beach, California (U.S.A.).

49. *Eventide,*
1982, oil, 72 × 72 cm.
Morro Bay, California.

50. *Texas Shrimpers,*
1984, oil, 48 × 72 cm.
Port Aransas, Texas.

51. *Dockside Reflections,*
1982, oil, 66 × 84 cm.
Astoria, Oregon.

52. *Fisherman's Wharf,*
1977, oil, 64 × 80 cm.
San Francisco, California.

JOYCE, MARSHALL W.

Portrayer of tall ships and the moods of the sea in oils and watercolor. In his youth, Joyce sailed the New England coast on a three-masted schooner skippered by his father. His grandfather, Capt. Marshall Woodside, was master of the full-rigged ship *Sintram*, a world-wide voyager.

Joyce paints the ten-year calendar series "Sailing Craft that Never Die" (a national award winner). His publications include "Dynamic Years", "20 Landscape Painters and How They Work" and "American Artist, February 1977".

Joyce has won several awards, the most recent of which: two Gold Medals of Honor from the Rockport Art Association (1974, 1982); Best of Show Award and Gold Medal of Honor from the New England Watercolor Society. He is member of the Guild of Boston Artists, the Key West, North Shore and Rockport Art Associations, New England Watercolor Society and the American Society of Marine Artists. He is affiliated with the following galleries: Trailside Galleries, Scottsdale, Arizona; Greenwich Gallery, Southport, Connecticut; Orleans Art Gallery; Annapolis Marine Art Gallery.

Born in Hertford, Massachusetts, 1912. Lives at 5 River Street, Kingston, Massachusetts (U.S.A.).

53. *Menemsha, Martha's Vineyard, south of Cape Cod,*
1980, watercolor, 44 × 60 cm.
This basin is lined with artists' shanties and galleries as well as fish houses. As home port to trawlers, lobsterboats and sportfishermen, it has managed to retain its working identity.

LAMBERT, CARL F. "NICK"

Lambert paints marine, architectural and aviation subjects, using a realistic technique. He is also self-employed as a risk management consultant in marine transportation and heavy construction.

Lambert studied under the Swiss artist Jean Jaques Pfister in Miami and Irving Shapiro, President of the American Academy of Art in Chicago.

Member of Midwest Watercolor Society and the American Society of Marine Artists, he has exhibited at the following venues: the Saint Louis Hotel, New Orleans; Navy Pier, Chicago; Mystic Seaport Gallery, Mystic; the Lake Michigan Maritime Museum, South Haven, Michigan; Grand Haven Community Center, Michigan. Lambert is currently affiliated with the Wren Gallery in Muskegon and his works may be found in corporate and private collections.

Born in Kansas City, Missouri, 1932. Lives at 575 Lake Forest Lane, Muskegon, Michigan (U.S.A.).

54. *Ready for Action,*
1986, watercolor, 26 × 34 cm.
Crisp spring weather at Wesley Marine in Montague, Michigan has local sailboats poised at the ready for a season of activity.

55. *Corporate Toys,*
1986, watercolor, 30 × 40 cm.
Some of the most beautiful yachts in the world find their way to Fort Lauderdale, Florida. The London ketch Thalassi is in the foreground at the Hotel Marriott Dock. Across the Intercoastal Canal at Pier 66 is a sleek motor yacht.

MANIER, YANNICK

The portrayal of the magical elements of sea and sail, elements which are impossible to render photographically, is Manier's forte. His watercolors possess all the qualities of purity and refinement inherent in all great works of art. He has a gift for making what is invisible, visible and what is intangible, tangible. All the characteristics of sailing in our epoch are collectively represented in any one of the artist's paintings.

The vessels Manier paints are often referred to as "phantom ships", but this does not solely derive from the fact that there is never a person to be seen on board. Like the Flying Dutchman, his boats derive their reality from the fact that they have substance in our imagination.

Eric Tabarly has said of his work "I find in Yannick Manier's paintings a marvellous world of sea and sailboats, realistically, precisely and poetically documented and painted in a way I have never seen before now: mindful of the construction and history of vessels I know well, all in their familiar settings."

Manier studied art at l'Académie Jullian and at l'Ecole Nationale des Arts et Métiers. He is an accomplished sailor and has made several lone voyages to the Indies, Polynesia and Tibet which have inspired a great many of his masterpieces.

He exhibits in Paris, Amsterdam, Milan, Geneva, Düsseldorf, Nantes and Concarneau and has collectors on five continents.

Born in Issy-les-Moulineaux, Haute-de-Seine, 1947. Lives at 5 rue Robert Estienne, Paris (France).

56. *En Course,*
1984, watercolor and gouache, 200 × 70 cm.

57. *Skoleirn,*
1986, watercolor and gouache, 70 × 50 cm.

58. *Rainbow and Endeavour,*
1984, watercolor and gouache, 240 × 80 cm.

MECRAY, JOHN

Mecray portrays the most famous of sailing yachts slicing through the waves with the cleanness and power which make big boat sailing so thrilling. He paints in oils and his sought after prints are made using the technique of grease and wax crayon on flat stone.

Much sailing and teaching experience has contributed to a unique multi-dimensional knowledge of boats and the demand of water and wind, perceived in every work. He is specialized in the painting of classic yachts and memorable sailing events and is best known for his sold-out limited edition prints of great racing yachts two of which were designated as the official commemorative prints of the 1980 and 1983 America's Cup defense.

Founder and chairman of the Museum of Yachting in Newport, Rhode Island and member of the New York and Fort Worth Boat Clubs, he is also member of the American Society of Marine Artists.

Born in Cape May, New Jersey, 1937. Lives at 24 Constellation Court, Jamestown, Rhode Island (U.S.A.).

59. *Shamrock V,*
1986, oil on linen, 42 × 98 cm.
Tea tycoon Sir Thomas Lipton's elegant America's Cup contender in 1930.

60. *Reliance,*
1983, oil on linen, 68 × 84 cm.
A 143 foot behemoth setting more sail on a single mast than any yacht in history. She was America's Cup defender in 1903, beating Shamrock III to the finish.

61. *Close-Hauled for the Finish, Westward and Britannia,*
1986, acrylic on linen, 52 × 92 cm.
The schooner Westward *met King George V's yacht* Britannia *in 1932 in European waters. They stormed across the finish line at Southsea in a dead heat.*

MISSEL, ESTHER B.

Specialized in the painting of tall ships, calm seas hold a special appeal for her as she considers painting light on sails and ships with all sails hoisted to be a challenge.

Missel graduated from Bay Path College in Longmeadow, Massachusetts, attended Wadsworth Atheneum School of Art in Hartford, Connecticut and studied fine art at Columbia University, New York.

As member of the American Artists Professional League Inc., the National League of American Pen Women: Women in Arts, the National Museum of Women in the Arts and the American Society of Marine Artists, Missel exhibits mainly at the Newman Galleries in Philadelphia and in the rotunda of the Cannon Building on Capitol Hill in Washington.

Born in Hartford, Connecticut, 1929. Lives at 264 East Main Street, Moorestown, New Jersey (U.S.A.).

62. *Dar Pomorza,*
acrylic, 59 × 83 cm.
Launched in 1909 and designed and built by Blohm & Voss, Hamburg, Dar Pomorza *originally sailed under the name of* Colbert *when laid up in France until 1918. She is currently owned by Museum Ship Dar Pomorza of Gydnia, Poland.*

63. *America II,*
acrylic, 59 × 83 cm.
In 1979, America II, *a replica of the original* America *of 100 Guinea Cup fame, was sold to Carlos Perdomo. She was resold in 1981 and is currently owned by Ramon Mendoza.*

MORRIS, ROGER

A special affinity for the sea, first-hand knowledge of ships and a passion for meticulous research has won international recognition for Morris's maritime paintings.

Morris was born into an artistic family: his father was a commercial artist and his mother, a portrait artist. The river Thames was his childhood playground. He started his apprenticeship to become a professional sailor as one of the custodians of the magnificent *Cutty Sark* and went on to train at Thames Nautical College H.M.S. Worcester.

On settling in New Zealand in 1960, Morris left the sea to train as a teacher and was also able to develop skills as a marine artist. In 1965, he began painting marine subjects in his spare time. In 1981, his book "Sail Change" (tall ships in New Zealand waters) was published, now sold out. He left teaching a year later to join the *Bounty* replica in Whangarei until mid 1984. He has since worked on the book "Pacific Sail" (European sailing ships in the Pacific from Magellan's time to the present), his second to be published by David Bateman Ltd.

Born in Berkshire, England, 1935. Lives in North Cove, Kawau Island, Warkworth (New Zealand).

64. *Spirit of New Zealand,*
1986, watercolor, 75 × 55 cm.
The vessel has been captured while clearing North Channel, Kawau Island. Astern is Takatu Point and the buoy marking Maori Rock, while in the distance Little Barrier Island is visible through the haze. Designed by Ewbank, Brooke & Co. and built by Thackwray Yachts Ltd of Auckland, this barquentine is one of New Zealand's sail training ships.

65. *Harbinger berthing Circular Quay. Sidney, circa 1890,*
1985, watercolor, 75 × 55 cm.
Built by Messrs. Steele & Co., Port Glasgow and launched in 1876, she was one of the loftiest ships of her time.

PARENT, YVES

Sailor, artist and executive, Parent may be the last of the Renaissance men. He owns a bottled mineral water company in Sainte Marguerite, Auvergne and when he's not being a businessman and when he's not painting, he's captaining his 36-foot sloop alone on transatlantic races.

Parent paints seascapes almost exclusively, and primarily in watercolor. He excels in the portrayal of placid waters dotted with boats, all in the most delicate of colors.

The artist participated in the Salon de Dessin et de la Peinture à l'Eau at the Grand Palais in Paris in 1982, 1984 and 1986 and in the Salon de la Marine in 1986. He exhibits at the following galleries in France: Estampille, Lille; Rollin, Rouen; La Plaisance, Honfleur; Raub, Brest; Le Chapitre, Rennes; Les Beaux-Arts, Vannes; Much, Nantes; Tissot, Arcachon; Emom, Paris. In the United States, he exhibits in: Annapolis, Maryland; Darien, Essex, Noank and Mystic, Connecticut; Marblehead, Massachusetts; Newport, Rhode Island; Portland, Maine.

Parent participated in all racing events organized by the Royal Ocean Racing Club between 1962 and 1966, the 1978 and 1982 Route du Rhum and the 1981-82 Whitbread Race. He has sailed in eight Fastnet races since 1963 and in various transatlantic races.

Born in Rouen, Normandy, 1941. Lives at Kerfrezec, Sainte Hélène, Hennebont (France).

66. *The Apparition of Benodet,*
1985, watercolor.

67. *Five Mile River After Rain,*
1985, watercolor.

PEARCE, LEONARD J.

Concentrates on historical marine subjects, sail and steam, and specific marine events. Pearce has revived the semi-transparent glazing technique (achieved by under painting in tempera and subsequently applying oil glazes on gessoed panels of mahogany or marine plywood) and warm colors popular in the 19th century. The artist studied at Sutton and Cheam School of Art and at City & Guilds in Kennington, London. He began his career in a design studio, working on architectural, graphic and product design projects. Since 1971, he has painted marine subjects in a traditional manner; formerly, under the name of 'John Bower'.

Pearce has prepared a series of twelve of "The Great 19th Century Clipper Ships" on fine porcelain and gilt plates for the Franklin Mint, 1982-84. He has exhibited at the Royal Society of Marine Artists and at the London International Boat Show. Since 1978, he has held one-man shows in the U.S.A. (Mystic Seaport Museum and Horton Point Lighthouse Museum, New York) and at the Swedish Maritime Museum. Examples of his paintings can be found in Mystic Seaport Museum (U.S.A.) permanent collection, the James Cook Museum, Middlesborough and the Institute of Naval Medicine in Portsmouth (U.K.).

Born in London, England, 1932. Lives at "Tyr-Graig", Argoed, Blackwood, Gwent, Wales (U.K.).

68. *Dreadnought,*
1982, oil, 62 × 42 cm.
Schooner yacht, designed by William Townsend and built in 1871 by C & R Poillon of New York. She is pictured with the New York Yacht Club fleet off the Sandy Hook Lightship.

69. *Arrow,*
1985, oil, 40 × 30.
Famous cutter of 84 tons built by Inman of Lymington for Joseph Weld of Lulworth Castle in 1821. She won the first cup given by the yacht club at Cowes, Isle of Wight, in 1826 and beat America in 1852.

PETERSON, PETE

Fascinated by the period of marine history from 1840 to 1930 (the transition from sail to steam), Peterson's paintings are based on a combination of places visited and scenarios gleaned from history books. In this sense, he strives to make his scenes 'fictitious but feasible'.

He is currently studying the Missouri and Mississippi rivers and their boats and ports. A self-taught artist, Peterson spent four years at sea with the U.S. Navy. He subsequently made a living doing drafting, mapping, geology, industrial designing and architecture while painting on the side. During this time, he was president of the Artists & Craftsman's Guild of Nevada for two years. He began painting full-time in 1971.

Peterson exhibits at Boen Gallery (Cape Garadeau), Gallery One (Denver), Cotton Stone Gallery (Jefferson), Jun Gallery (Philadelphia), Kathleen's Gallery (Atlanta) and American Design Ltd (Denver).

Peterson's art hangs in various public collections, including: Everson Museum of Fine Arts, New York; Holdorado Western Art Museum, Las Vegas; Petro Lewis Oil Company, Denver; Port Everglades Pilot's Association, Fort Lauderdale.

Born in Denver, 1931. Lives at 17 N. 4th Street, Columbia, Mendocino (U.S.A.).

70. *Columbia and Shamrock I,*
oil, 72 × 96 cm.
A scene from America's Cup 1899.

71. *Courageous and Australia,*
oil, 72 × 96 cm.
A scene from America's Cup 1977.

POHLMANN, ERNST

Accomplished etcher, marine painter and graphic artist since 1961, Pohlmann's inborn love of the sea and sailing has endowed him with a very personal approach to marine art. His style is precise and unpretentious and this simplicity is reflected in his choice of muted colors, so typical of northern waters.

Most of Pohlmann's works depict beach scenes, piers, islands, sailing and fishing boats. His watercolors and sketches are brought back from frequent voyages aboard his yacht *Jutta.*

In 1947, Pohlmann left his native Magdeburg for Wolfsburg in the Federal Republic of Germany. There, he studied under Herman Rohrmann, renowned restorer and church painter of the times. His early studies were consolidated in Braunschweig where he worked in the Gerlinde Huck workshops, perfecting his knowledge of artisan printing techniques.

Pohlmann is a member of the Berufsverband Bildender Künstler of Hamburg and exhibits at a series of small galleries, prefering more personalized ambiences for his paintings; these include: Kunsthaus, Galerie Mensch, Ludwig-Erhardt-Haus and Museum für Hamburgische Geschichte in Hamburg and Deutscher Schiffahrtsmuseum and Morgensternmuseum in Bremerhaven. Other venues include Friedrichshafen, Bodensee and Hiswa in Amsterdam.

Born in Vahldorf, Magdeburg, 1936. Lives at Fahrenort 10, Hamburg (Germany).

72. *Altenwerder Kutter Greta im Watt,*
watercolor etching, 13 × 15 cm.

73. *Lampenfischer,*
watercolor etching, 12 × 30 cm.

REYNOLDS, KEITH L.

Full-time artist since 1961, Reynolds goes straight to the essentials, so his yachts and workboats are like meticulously detailed ship models floating serenely in a vast evocative space.

He spent his early years on Puget Sound, Seattle, on fishing boats, tugs and ferries that later would become the subjects of his painting. He subsequently studied fine art at the University of Oregon and graduated in professional arts at the Art Center College of Design where he worked under Al King, developer of the tri-color system. Reynolds then went on to be president of his own film production company and design consultant to cultural institutions such as the Smithsonian Institute, Colonial Williamsburg and the Hayden Planetarium. The artist is an award winning member of the Society of Illustrators, New York, and multiple award winner in the Mystic Outdoor Art Festival. As member of the American Society of Marine Artists, he exhibits on a national level, particulary at the Slater and Mariners' Museums.

Born in Seattle, Washington, 1929. Lives at 46 W. Mystic Avenue, Mystic, Connecticut (U.S.A.).

74. *Morning on the Aegean Sea,*
acrylic, 34 × 68 cm.
Just off the island of Mykonos, these small fishing craft sit in the quiet rising heat of an August morning. They are typical of the marvellous variety of boats that still work these waters.

75. *Volunteer,*
14 color serigraph printed on 100% rag paper, neutral ph, 32 × 52 cm.
Volunteer was the American defender in the 1887 America's Cup. She was converted to a schooner four years later.

76. *Ghosting Along,*
12 color serigraph printed on 100% rag paper, neutral ph, 50 × 36 cm.
Originally inspired by a sailboat cutting away from the viewers' flotilla after the first racing day of the America's Cup in 1983.

ROBINSON, CHARLES R.

Painter of the graceful and historic, but still active, Chesapeake Bay sailing log canoes in particular and of the waters of the Maine coast in general.

Exposed to art at an early age, Robinson was influenced by Howard Pyle, the Wyeths and all artists belonging to the Brandywine School. He studied under Daniel Greene, the late Robert Beverly Hale and Robert Brackman, and also painted with John Howard Sanden.

Robinson has rowed 2,000 miles down the Ohio and Mississippi rivers to the Gulf of Mexico and 4,500 miles up the Amazon and its tributaries. During college he founded the Colonial Arms Foundry, a company that manufactured model operational reproductions of U.S. Naval cannon of the 1812 vintage. These cannon appear in the permanent collections of the Philadelphia Maritime Museum and the Chesapeake Bay Maritime Museum.

Robinson is life member of the Art Students League, New York, active in the National Maritime History Society and South Street Seaport Museum, and chartered artist, member, officer and director of the American Society of Marine Artists. The Peabody Museum of Massachusetts and The Mariners' Museum of Virginia have exhibited his works. He has also been featured in several publications, including "Nautical Quarterly", "Sea History", "Yankee Magazine" and "Architectural Digest".

Born in Pennsylvania, 1940. Lives at Brush Hill Studios, Washington, Connecticut (U.S.A.).

77. *Black Can,*
1980, oil, 84 × 96 cm.
Forbes Magazine Collection, New York.

78. *Starboard Tack,*
1981, oil, 42 × 60 cm.
Mr Jack E. Brown, Texas.
Governor's Cup 1980. Pictured at historic St. Michael's on the eastern shore of Maryland is the Billie P. Hall *in the distance on a starboard tack while the crew of the* Mystery *hikes out on the 'spring boards' in response to a fresh breeze.*

RUSSELL, R.E.

Sensitivity for beauty and serenity has earned Russell the title "Poet of the Palette". A romanticist, he attempts to capture that rare fleeting moment we remember long after more dynamic scenes are forgotten: the silhouette of a solitary figure atop a cliff, the reflection of a sailboat in oily-calm waters, a seagull about to settle on a buoy. The artist deliberately avoids exaggerated accuracy so that all his paintings have a timeless quality about them. He reserves a particular fascination for the Orient; although his renderings are far from typical, they still possess the qualities of the Far East.

A professional artist, Russell attended the Swaine School of Design in New Bedford, Massachusetts and the University of Kansas. His works hang in private collections throughout America and abroad and are on display at galleries in Honolulu, San Francisco and Carmel. Member of the American Society of Marine Artists, he regularly exhibits at the Laguna Beach Festival of Arts and Laguna Beach Sawdust Festival.

Born in Brooklyn, New York, 1933. Lives at 3089 Bern Drive, Laguna Beach, California (U.S.A.).

79. *Lady Char,*
1986, oil, 60 × 120 cm.
A Riva commissioned by Fred Gamm, Huntingdon Beach, California.

80. *Old Loves,*
1986, oil, 32 × 40 cm.
A 1937 Chris Craft and 1937 Packard, both owned and commissioned by Hatteras broker Rod Hageman, Newport Beach, California.

STICKER, ROBERT E.

A colorful visual storyteller and careful researcher who has given enduring life to the legends and achievements of whaleships and sailing navies.

Sticker lived on Staten Island for forty-five years, attended Brooklyn College and C.C.N.Y. and served as naval aviator and patrol plane commander (flying boats) during World War II. He then worked for seventeen years for California Texas Oil Company. He has been painting professionally since 1963, having studied drawing and painting at the Art Students League with Frank Reilly. The artist is currently painting a series of prints documenting the importance of the riverboat in the settling of America.

Sticker is associated with Grand Central Art Galleries since 1964 and is founding member of the American Society of Marine Artists. Sticker's pictures are in the collections of I.B.M., National Distillers, Vesuvius Crucible Company, Albert Lowe Museum in the Bahamas and the Franklin Mint. He was awarded the Franklin Mint Marine Contest Gold Medal.

Born in Jersey City, New Jersey, 1922. Lives at R.D. 1, Pleasant Mount, Pennsylvania (U.S.A.).

81. *Pittsburgh in the Seventies,*
watercolor, 35 × 60 cm.
Riverboat Alice Brown *in the 1870s, where the Monongahela and Allegheny Rivers meet to form The Golden Triangle.*

82. *The Royal George,*
watercolor, 36 × 48 cm.
Launched for the British Navy in 1756, and graced with one of the more elaborate examples of the art of the figure-head carver, she was famous for having capsized at Spithead in 1782 with a loss of 900 lives.

The rare luminosity of Thompson's work is primarily the result of a painstaking technique practised by the Van de Veldes and later by the 19th century masters of marine art. Applying layers of thin translucent oil washes, the colors are carefully blended and the detail laid on so cleverly it is hard to find a break in the smooth finished surface of the canvas.

Born in Hull, England in 1951, Thompson spent much of his childhood on the island of Herm in the Channel Islands, where, intrigued by the moods of the sea, he taught himself to paint. He returned to England in 1973 to take up horticulture but, following an accident in 1979, he began painting full-time. In just a few years he has become a leading marine artist with his paintings sought by collectors around the world. Thompson has recently finished a three year commission to paint scenes from all twenty-six Challenges for the America's Cup. Fifteen of these have now been reproduced as prints, details of which may be obtained by writing to the artist at Ashcombe Tower, Dawlish, Devon (England).

83. *Resolute defeats Shamrock IV,* 1986, oil, 44 × 60 cm.
America's Cup 1920. Shamrock IV, *generally known as 'the ugly duckling', and* Resolute, *which is pointing higher and taking her wind, battle it out in the crucial third race of a very close series.*

84. *Defender defeats Valkyrie III,* 1985, oil, 44 × 60 cm.
America's Cup 1895. The topmast of the crippled yacht Defender *leans drunkenly backwards towards her port side as* Valkyrie III *bears away having carried away a stay with the end of her boom at the start of the second race.*

85. *Columbia defeats Shamrock,* 1984, oil, 44 × 60 cm.
America's Cup 1899. Described at the time as 'the finest fifteen mile run in history', the two yachts sweep along in the deciding third race while many spectator boats fly 'the Shamrock' in recognition of Sir Thomas Lipton.

MARINE ART INSTITUTIONS REFERRED TO IN THIS BOOK

American Society of Marine Artists, 212 Second Ave., Milford, CT 06460, U.S.A.
Annapolis Marine Art Gallery, 110 Dock St., City Dock, Annapolis, MD 21401, U.S.A.
Arnold Art Gallery, 210 Thames St., Newport, R.I. 02840, U.S.A.
Calvert Marine Museum, Solomons Island, Maryland, U.S.A.
Canadian Society of Marine Artists, 2801 Lyndene Road, N. Vancouver, B.C. V3S 4N8, Canada.
Chesapeake Bay Maritime Museum, St. Michaels, Maryland, U.S.A.
Deutsches Schiffahrtsmuseum, Bremerhaven, Bremen Deutschland.
Franklin Mint Gallery, Franklin, PA 19091, U.S.A.
Grand Central Art Galleries, 24 West 57th St., New York, N.Y. 10019, U.S.A.
Greenwich Workshop Gallery, 2600 Post Road, Southport, CT 06490, U.S.A.
Herreshoff Marine Museum, Bristol, Rhode Island, U.S.A.
Horton Point Lighthouse Museum, Long Island, New York, U.S.A.
Institute of Naval Medicine, Portsmouth, England.
James Cook Museum, Middlesborough, England.
John Stobart Gallery, Union Wharf, Boston, MA 02109, U.S.A.
Kirsten Gallery, 5320 Roosevelt Way N.E., Seattle, WA 98105, U.S.A.
Lake Michigan Maritime Museum, South Haven, Michigan, U.S.A.

Morgensternmuseum, Bremerhaven, Bremen, Deutschland.
Museum für Hamburgische Geschichte, Hamburg, Deutschland.
Mystic Maritime Gallery, Mystic Seaport Museum Stores, Mystic, CT 06355, U.S.A.
National Maritime Museum, Greenwich, London SE10 GNF, England.
Nautical Heritage Museum, Dana Point, California, U.S.A.
Navy Art Collection, 1311 Delaware Ave. S.W., Washington, DC 20024, U.S.A.
Navy Combat Museum, Washington, D.C., U.S.A.
Newman Galleries, 1625 Walnut St., Philadelphia, PA 19103, U.S.A.
Newman & Saunders Galleries, 120 Bloomingdale Ave., Wayne, PA 19087, U.S.A.
Noroton Gallery, Darien, Connecticut, U.S.A.
Nya Varvet Naval Port, Göteborg, Sverige.
Peabody Museum of Salem, Salem, Massachusetts, U.S.A.
Royal Navy Museum, Portsmouth, England.
Royal Society of Marine Artists, 17 Carlton House Terrace, London SW1 5BD, England.
Salmagundi Club, 47 Fifth Ave., N.Y. 10003, U.S.A.
Sjöfartsmuseet, Göteborg, Sverige.
Society of Illustrators Museum of American Illustration, 128 East 63rd St., N.Y. 10021, U.S.A.
South Street Seaport Museum, New York, U.S.A.
The Mariners' Museum, Newport News, Virginia, U.S.A.